SWINTON
A WALK IN THE PAST

To Allan. with love
April 1997.

I am sure this will bring
back Memories!

Joan.

SWINTON
A WALK IN THE PAST

MICHAEL JOHN FOWLER

Wharncliffe Publishing Limited

**First Published in 1996 by
Wharncliffe Publishing Limited**

Copyright © Michael John Fowler 1996

*For up-to-date information on other titles produced under the
Wharncliffe imprint, please telephone or write to:*

**Wharncliffe Publishing Limited
FREEPOST
47 Church Street
Barnsley
South Yorkshire S70 2BR
Telephone (24 hours): 01226 - 734555**

ISBN: 1-871647-30-4

A CIP catalogue record of this book is available from the
British Library.

Printed in Great Britain by Redwood Books, Trowbridge,
Wiltshire

CONTENTS

ACKNOWLEDGMENTS

I owe much of the project to Mr Tom Oliver, of Highfield Road, without whose initial invaluable help, and loan of many of the photographs, would have meant this would never have come off the drawing – or should I say – writing board. I am also deeply indebted to Mr Jack Ardron, of Kilnhurst, for correcting my technical errors and for the private viewing of the most fascinating historical slide show I have ever seen. Also for the unselfish loan of part of his own photographic collection, to complete this book.

Other thanks go to Geoff Wharnes of Doncaster for his colour shots, to enable me to compile the Mexborough and Swinton Traction Company section. To Jack Marshall for the Pottery, Chris and Pearl Sharp ('Old Barnsley') for some beautifully detailed photographs of Swinton's early period. Finally to David Simm for his design of the jacket.

INTRODUCTION

The very first recorded mention of Swinton appears in the Domesday survey, which was completed in 1086, twenty years after the Battle of Hastings. It is strongly believed however, that parts of the area were inhabited during Roman times, from the discovery of earthworks, which run through Kimberworth, Greasbrough, and Haugh to Swinton Common and Piccadilly, and on towards Wentworth Park. This is further supported by a historical find in 1853, of a vase containing approximately three hundred Roman coins, dating from 69 to 212 AD., in the Rockingham Road area, close to the Woodman Inn.

The name of Swinton originates from the Old English for 'the Swine Farm', as in the Domesday book, it was described as an area of mainly pasture and waste woodland. Further to this, early Medieval documents refer Swinton as 'Villa Porcorum', which is Latin for 'House of Pigs', crudely confirming the previous description.

Although it did have its own chapel in Norman times there is no mention of a church, probably because of the so few inhabitants. For well over seven hundred years Swinton was part of the Parish of Wath and as such the Church following was in that town. In fact until 1817, the people of Swinton had to be buried in Wath. One such large burial was in 1646 when a third of its population were wiped out by the Plague, the remains of which were uncovered in 1913, when the new Church Hall at Wath was excavated.

It remained as a large village, with some 146 houses, until about 1804, when it became a recognised junction town, through the construction and opening of the Dove & Dearne canal, which linked the Don navigation to the Barnsley canal. There is little doubt that this was an initial factor in bringing about Swinton's industrial development. New work in the form of boat building and repairing began, and other industries quickly followed, including the addition of a new pottery - The Don, to complement the Rockingham Pottery, at the opposite end of the town.

Close to the canal system more industry began, including an Iron Foundry, linked to the Don Pottery; The Don Chemical Works and Swinton Iron Works; and The Glass Works (Dale Brown & Co. Ltd).

The population however remained under 2,000 until the development of Manvers and Wath Main Colliery when people began to flood into the area. More and more Collieries opened nearby and in the span of just 50 years a further 10,000 people had moved into the locality of Swinton.

By 1901 it was a bustling town with a wide variety of employment and industry, which included an active Railway network, running through its centre. But it was ill prepared for its expansion and facilities such as water, sanitation and electricity were totally inadequate. Work began on several new drainage systems, the development of existing wells and a sewerage works, and with the addition of electricity, in 1907 a tramway was added to improve links with other towns. In a relatively short period of time Swinton began to cope with its growth.

Today, in 1996, Swinton is still developing. New estates are being added. Even with the disastrous set-back of the destruction of the Collieries – once the main life-blood of employment in the 20th Century – things are beginning to re-develop. New funding has arrived and smaller industries are employing again, with the added attraction of a cleaner environment. As for the main town itself, old parts still survive, with its terraced housing standing side-by-side neat semis. The older detached houses have been refurbished and woods and farmland are still not too far away.

The Fitzwilliam Family are still an important remembrance, and testimony to them are the existence of the streets of Fitzwilliam and Milton, as well as the school. Without doubt their support in the distant past has ensured Swinton has a future.

The following pages of photographs and description expands on some of the text contained within this introduction, giving a better insight, and hopefully fond memories on the way, into much of Swinton's past and development.

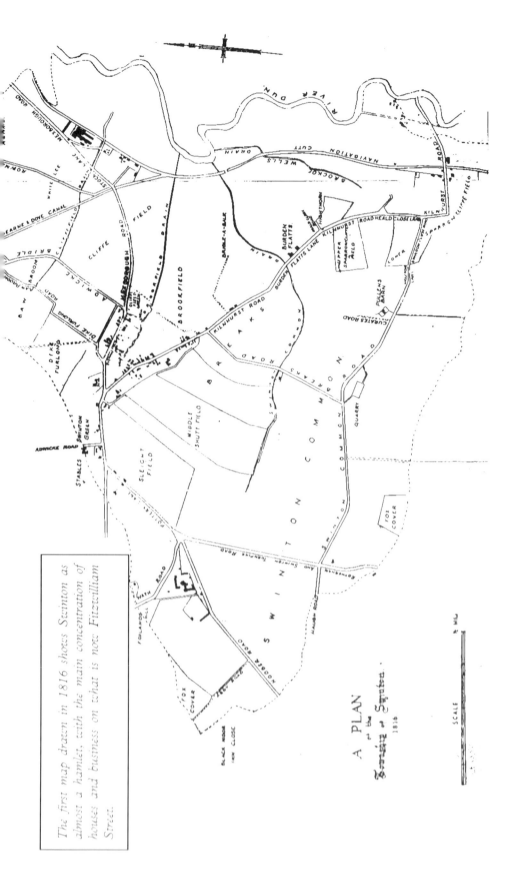

The first map drawn in 1816 shows Stainton as almost a hamlet, with the main concentration of houses and business on what is now Fitzwilliam Street.

A PLAN
of the
Township of Swinton.
1816

SCALE

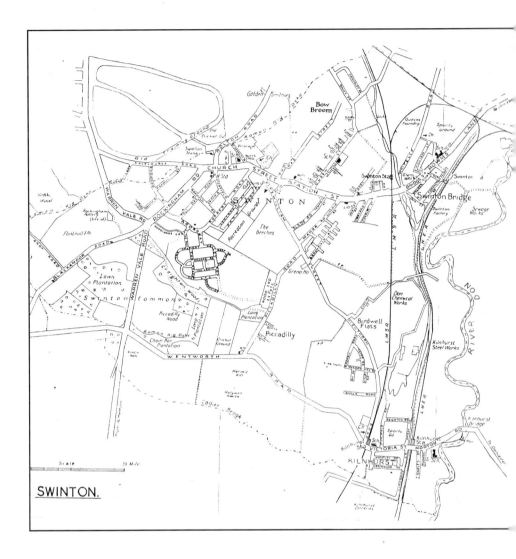

SWINTON.

Many of the road names were changed prior to the drawing of the second map in 1954: Rotherham and Swinton turnpike has become Warren Vale Road; Hoober Road is now Blackamoor Road; Pottery Lane is Rockingham Road; Mexborough Road is Station Street; Brecks Road is Piccadilly Road; Kilnhurst Road is Fitzwilliam Street, and Swinton Common Road is now Wentworth Road. Also many new estates have developed to form Swinton into a recognised town.

Rockingham Pottery

In 1745 Edward Butler established a Pottery works on land owned by the Marquis of Rockingham. The advantage to this location was that Swinton had local clay, coal was available from a nearby Colliery, and a quarry at Wath, provided stone for the buildings.

Butler was not a man of means, but a simple potter who worked hard to establish a business. Subsequently, after twenty years, the works were taken over by various proprietors and the Swinton Pottery works began to enlarge as demand for the wares increased.

From 1787 the business passed into the hands of the Green family, a well known Pottery family of Leeds. However partnership difficulties arose and the firm was handed over to the Brameld brothers - William and John. With their business acumen, trade expanded and the works were further extended and at its height was employing some 300 local people. The two brothers had three sons between them and the business was passed down to them. These brothers worked extremely hard and began experimenting to improve the quality of the product, which included engaging artists for new

In this photograph of the kiln, note the outbuilding attached when it was converted to provide a suitable dwelling for a family to reside for many years. Entrance was up a small flight of steps to the left.

Right: *The kiln today.*

designs. Very soon some of the finest pottery was being produced.

About 1820 money difficulties arose through their efforts to produce the finest quality wares, from the dearest clay. Creditors were quickly looming, but the Earl of Fitzwilliam became the Potteries saviour. He was so impressed with their examples, he provided the necessary capital to continue production. In gratitude, the works were renamed The Rockingham Pottery, and it became the most important business in the entire district.

In a relatively short period of time, - between 1826 and 1842, - porcelain produced at Rockingham was being shipped to Russia and many European Countries. Also large quantities were made for Royalty and Nobility, as well as the Earl of Fitzwilliam himself.

The ultimate accolade was the designing of a 200 piece dinner service for His Majesty King William IV, which was shipped individually to London. It was this striving for perfection however, that became the firms undoing, and in 1842, after struggling financially for several years, the works closed. They never re-opened.

The brothers did continue to live locally until their deaths and are now buried in Swinton graveyard.

Today Rockingham Pottery is a very much sought after antique, with many fine collections in private hands as well as museums.

This once prosperous industry is also remembered locally with the surrounding streets of Rockingham, Griffin (Its hallmark design) and Brameld.

When the Pottery buildings began falling apart, and prior to demolition, the last remaining kiln of three – The Waterloo Kiln – (named from the Napoleonic Wars) had a small shed and room attached to it. It was initially used as an isolation hospital for smallpox patients. This was not for too long a period and once it had become vacant, a family moved in and actually lived in the kiln until 1951.

In the 1970's the local Council cleared the last remaining parts of the Rockingham works and seeded the area. They did however repair and return the Waterloo kiln to its former state. This now stands amongst the trees as a constant reminder to the former glory of Rockingham.

Below is a fine example of one of the Pottery's many wares which were produced during Rockingham's heyday.

Pottery Farm, Blackamoor Lane

Pottery Farm was situated on land just below the Rockingham Pottery works and was used as stables for the horses who worked within the pottery. When the Rockingham works closed the farm concentrated on working the land and dealing in dairy products.

It was worked until 1977, but because of its dilapidated condition the owner had to leave. It quickly became vandalised and the derelict farm was demolished only a few years later.

In the second photograph below, one can see its relative locality to the old Rockingham works, with the last remaining kiln and house in view. The house has recently undergone additions which has changed the character of the building.

A herd of cows are being returned from pasture, along Blackamoor Lane, for milking. In the distance is an area known as the Woodman (circa 1950).
Inset: *The same location today with a roundabout at the end of the road.*

Gamekeeper's Stake Hut, Creighton Woods

With the building of the Highfields Farm Estate, in the 1940's, by Swinton Council, they wanted to add more pleasant surroundings to the properties. And so in 1948 they purchased 22 acres of woodland from Earl Fitzwilliam. They developed this into a beautiful one mile walk, and called it 'Creighton Woods' in honour of the family who were head gardeners to Earl Fitzwilliam living nearby the woods.

The old gamekeeper's stake hut that abutts onto the wood. The framework of this building still exists because when the land was sold and a dwelling erected, the builders actually incorporated it into an extension of the house.

Woodmans Inn

There has been much change over the years, since the 'Woodmans Inn' was built, just before the turn of the century, by Wath based Whitworth's Brewery. At one time a butchers shop used to operate

from a tiny room at the back of the public house. When the brewery closed the public house was taken over by Barnsley Brewery, the 's' was dropped from its name and the butcher's shop was forced to close.

The Woodman Inn is now owned by John Smith's Brewery and both the inside and outside have been completely refurbished.

Rockingham Road

This row of cottages stood at the junction with Brameld Road. They have all been demolished and new semi-detached houses built on the plots. The white building to the far right is now a Chinese take-away.

Kings Head, Rockingham Road

An 18th century public house situated just above the Gate Inn. The current licensee, Mr. Tom Stead, was born and bred in this pub, when it was run by his Father.

Tom joined the Royal Navy and upon his retirement went into the Licensing trade. His first place was in Mexborough, but when the King's Head tenancy became available, he grasped at the opportunity to return to 'his home'.

Racecourse Road

Although I have titled this Racecourse Road, when the above photograph was taken it was not a road as such, merely a dirt track that ran parallel with the racecourse. This is taken looking towards Swinton common and the new-looking building with the tall chimney is in fact the old waterworks pumping station, which no longer exists.

Inset: Today's view of the Racecourse. The waterworks have been demolished and the wasteland remains an eyesore.

Swinton Stables and Racecourse

The love of horse racing is an hereditary trait in many Yorkshire families, none more than the Earl of Fitzwilliam, whose descendants also owned and bred many fine horses, training many of them at his stables near Golden Smithies Lane. His horses also ran in the name of the Earl's son, Viscount Milton.

In 1857 The Swinton Club was founded and a few race meetings were held at Swinton, where there was an exceptionally fine course. The race meetings were only few and the stables were used, in the main, for horse-training.

In the early 1900's pressure was being placed on Swinton because of a large influx of workers who were flocking to the area for the new Collieries that were emerging, and a new housing stock was required.

The stables were emptied and sold and private developers moved in to construct many new dwellings. A new estate and road was developed, part of that road passed through the old straight of the racing track and was named Racecourse Road.

The entrance way to these fine stables was off Golden Smithies

A view from Swinton Common down Golden Smithies Lane. To the left is the entrance way to the Stables. This roadway still exists but provides access to a brand-new housing estate(inset). Below: The front archways of the old stable block on the racecourse just prior to demolition.

Lane and is now the roadway to a brand-new private housing estate, called The Stables.

The houses on the far right of the aerial photograph, and the bungalow's at the top right, still exist.

Wardle's Farm, Swinton Common

Norman 'Peggy' Wardle's farm was situated on the junction of Golden Smithies Lane and Church Street. The entire farm, through age, had to be demolished and this area is now the car park for the Gate Inn. The row of buildings in the background are part of Swinton Stables.

Above: Norman 'Peggy' Wardle's farm before demolition. Note the sign on the post directing persons to the nearest air-raid shelter. Inset: The scene from the same spot now.

Detail of the outbuildings to the far left of the farm before they were knocked down.

The Toll House Swinton Common

Like many other towns in England, Swinton had its own toll gate, which was situated on the main Rotherham to Doncaster Road, by the junction of Golden Smithies Lane. It was just below a Coaching House, aptly named the Gate Inn.

Although the toll gate was removed in the 19th Century the hexagonal shaped Toll House remained for well into the 20th Century, as a dwelling. Its location on the map is referred to as Swinton Common. However older residents in the area actually call the locality 'The Toll Bar.'

In this photograph some new buildings are under construction, in the background. These are the current row of shops on the Common, which includes the Post Office.

The Toll House was demolished shortly after the shops were completed but the outline of its original shape can still be faintly seen beneath the tarmac frontage.

The old Toll Gate House; usual octagonal construction with a centre-placed chimney. This area formed the living quarters and the attached smaller construction the bedroom. It was used as a residence well into this century.

Gate Inn

This series of photographs clearly demonstrates how, in the time frame of ninety years, one small area undergoes dramatic changes. Using the Gate Inn as the focal point note how in the second picture, taken in the thirties, the Inn has received an overall plaster facing and the photograph has been retouched, removing the chimney and trees. Thirty years later and the area has become built up with the road metalled; tram lines have disappeared but overhead cables remain to power trolley buses. In the modern *now* picture note the bus in the approximate postion of the tram in the first picture — thus completing this travel-through-time sequence.

Swinton Common, Church Street

Two further views of the Swinton Common location. The first (above) is taken from the Gate Inn, looking down towards the town centre. The row of shops and the Post Office are to the left. The zebra crossing has now been replaced by a more up-to-date pelican crossing.

The photograph below is looking up towards the Common area. The building top, centre, is the old Police station.

The first house, to the left, has now been demolished and a shop has been built, slightly back off the road. The other cottages, where the group of boys are, still exist, though no longer as dwellings.

Inset: The scene present-day, the one-storey building has lost a window and chimney.

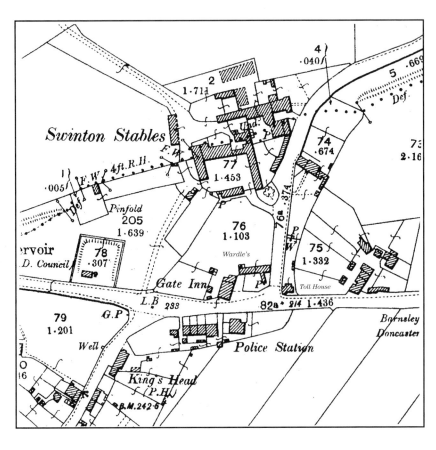

Map of Swinton Common showing the location of Swinton Stables, Wardle's Farm, The Gate Inn and the Toll House.

Church Street

Swinton Fitzwilliam, Junior and Infant School

Built in 1860 thanks to a large donation by The Earl of Fitzwilliam, it provided schooling for both Infant and Junior school children. However in the early 1950's overcrowding was causing disruption, and after much representation, work began on an infant school on Rookery Road. Pupils moved into that school in 1952, leaving this old building as just a Junior school.

In 1978 a new Junior school was also completed on Rookery Road, next to the Infants, and after 125 years the school closed.

The school has seen a few sportsmen emerge, with Sheffield

United footballer's, Geoff Salmons and Frank Barlow, showing off their first ball control skills here.

The school was sold two years after closing, and has now been developed into a large dwelling house and a number of luxury flats.

Airey's shop, Church Street

Mrs Airey lived in the end house, to the right of the top photograph, and had her front room converted into a shop. It was always open for daily necessities, or even just to 'nip in' for local news and gossip.

More importantly, it was directly opposite Swinton Fitzwilliam school and children would sneak across at dinner-time for some 'spice.'

The bottom photograph is taken at the rear of these buildings

Ring O'Bells, Church Street

No one quite knows why it is called The Ring O'Bells, but with St. Margaret's Church opposite, this may be the answer, for the bells still peal out loudly every Sunday. This 18th Century public house, although retaining its low beamed ceilings, has been modernised both inside and out.

The building next to it standing slightly back is the old blacksmiths. This has since been demolished and a group of modern shops have been built.

The white house above and centre is the corner house of the old 'Rookery.' This is now the 'Peace gardens.'

Right: The Ring O'Bells today.

'The Rookery'

These five photographs show a cluster of cottages which all made up 'The Rookery', aptly named because of its proximity to the Churchyard rookery which was across the road. This group of houses stood at the corner of what is now Rookery Road and Church Street.

These have long since been demolished and the land left behind is now the 'Peace Gardens.'

This view of Church Street dates to before 1907, when the tram lines arrived. The edge of the white cottage to the left is part of the 'rookery' and the house above is just below 'coffin row', (these have all now gone). To the right are the fine Victorian houses of Butts Terrace and just above, in the centre, is Fitzwilliam Junior and Infants School.

Church Street

The whole of Butts Terrace. The veranda along its frontage has now been removed.

The photograph below is of a row of houses which once stood above the 'Rookery' to Butts Terrace. With the first pair you can see part of the newly constructed Peace Gardens to the left. The row going out right was known as 'Coffin Row' because of its shape.

St Margaret's Church, Church Street

St. Margaret's Church - Church Street. With the Norman Chapel dilapidating rapidly, at the beginning of the 19th Century, and an increasing population, it was apparent that a new Church for the Parish of Swinton was required. And so under the Patronage of the

St. Margaret's Church before the fire of 1897

Earl of Fitzwilliam, the Church of St. Margarets was built in 1817.

The interior however was sadly lacking in decent furnishings, with many of the pews supplied by the wealthy parishioners for only their own use, and so by 1890 a restoration scheme was planned, and put into action for the raising of funds.

By 1897 tenders had been invited to carry out the restoration work, but on March the 24th that year, the Church was nearly destroyed by a raging fire.

It was a cold March, with a biting wind, and therefore a heating apparatus was lit in the early afternoon ready for the evening service. The vicar left the Church to go about his business and it was whilst he was absent that disaster struck. It is believed that a spark from a defective flue started the blaze.

Shortly after 4 o'clock that afternoon, the alarm was raised by two Police Officers patrolling the area, who saw smoke billowing from one of the windows. The Swinton fire brigade, with their horse drawn carriage, were quickly on the scene, but unfortunately their equipment was badly in need of repair, and hosing repeatedly burst.

The pews burned quickly and fiercely and consequently, within half an hour, the entire roof had caved in.

Added support from Mexborough and Rotherham's Fire brigade came but the blaze had taken well hold. A further problem arose when it was realised that the fire-hoses were not long enough to reach

the high belfry.   It was feared the whole Church would soon be engulfed in the inferno.

Then with great courage, two firemen from Mexborough, slung a ladder against the walls of the belfry and hauled buckets of water up to douse the timbers inside. They managed to save the Tower.

In a moment of respite, whilst the firemen dampened down the remains, the villages who had gathered to watch the spectacle, heard the Church clock striking 6 o'clock. In less than two hours only four bare walls and the tower were standing.

A collection to rebuild the Church began immediately, with sightseeing villagers, contributing towards the new St. Margaret's.

The shape of the new building, incorporating the old tower, was to be slightly larger, and one year later the first foundation stone was laid.

By 1899 the present St. Margaret's was complete.

A local resident, who became a teacher at Swinton Fitzwilliam school, and who sadly is no longer with us, recorded her early memories of St. Margaret's Church, in a small document form. The following is an extract from her early life at the age of six, when she recollected the great Church fire:

At the time I was recovering from a particularly sharp attack of bronchitis and neither Mother nor I had been out for weeks. About tea time on the Wednesday afternoon a strange commotion arose on the streets. Lots of people came hurrying out of their homes and went up the town. Mother dare not go out to investigate lest I should follow and so it was not until later in the evening that Mother heard the cause of it all. Children coming out of the old "top school" (National – to give it its proper name) at 4 p.m. began shouting "Church is on fire, Church is on fire". The late Mr.C.W.H. Peat, the then headmaster – a staunch and loyal Churchman – came out to see whatever they meant, and was shocked to see the Church well alight. He immediately got in touch with Rotherham Fire Brigade and I have been told that in 30 minutes they were tackling the fire. That seems an incredibly short time as in those days all vehicles were horse drawn, and at that time there was very little traffic on the road, so that the brigade would have a clear run.

On the Thursday morning the late Dr. Blythman called to see his patient and found her so much better that he said if there were no setbacks, and the weather was suitable, I could go out the following Sunday.

Sunday came, and it was an incredibly lovely day – warm. sunny with beautiful sky and fleecy white clouds. In the afternoon I was well wrapped up and Mother and I went to see the ruined Church.

As we went up the Churchyard I don't remember the Church looking very much different from what it had always done. But when I got inside!. The porch was terribly dirty and littered, and the Church itself almost indescribable. The ground – there was no floor left, was full of rubble and debris. We climbed rather than walked about. Of the Church there was nothing but four charred, blackened, roofless walls and a cracked tower. People were talking in hushed tones. Mother was crying and could only nod or shake her head when spoken to, and I gripped her hand feeling very frightened. Men had taken off their hats. I wondered why?

A group of men looking in the tower – it is on the east side – were speaking rather louder. I remember some of their comments. "Tower will have to come down, they'll ne'er patch a crack like that up". "It wouldn't be safe to leave the tower standing with a crack like that in it" etc. etc.

Thank God the crack was mended and the same tower still stands, for it is a particularly fine one of its type.

When we came out a man was standing in the doorway, holding out his hat and sightseers were dropping coins into it.

When the Norman Chapel was ready for demolition, concerned followers had the archway and old buttercross moved from Chapel Hill up to St. Margaret's Churchyard and rebuilt behind the church.

The new interior after rebuilding work.

Sadly the old archway has now crumbled and only a pile of stones remain. The old buttercross has been moved to its present location, next to the Church main doors.

Below: *The old vicarage which was replaced with a new house.*

Farm Lane

This dirt pathway was also known as T'old Lane and was regularly used as a short cut by miners walking to Manvers Main Colliery. This lane later became St. John's Road.

This photograph is facing towards Church Street – the main road.

The farm belonging to Thomas Sharpley, to the left has now been demolished and the grassland left behind is part of Chapel Hill. The barn to the left still remains and is owned by Nelson's Electrical.

Sharpley's Farm Chapel Hill

This is the rear of Thomas Sharpley's farm on Chapel Hill, which was demolished when St.John's Road was constructed. (The area is now grassed over).

Tom's farm was not a big affair, just a smallholding, dealing mainly in eggs and milk from his own cattle and poultry.

The Sharpley brothers were all well known businessmen in town. Jim owned and ran a smallholding on Fitzwilliam Road, near Manor Road (photo below) whilst Albert owned a butchery business on Bridge Street, opposite the Don Hotel.

Jim Sharpley's farm was situated on the corner of Fitzwilliam Street and Manor Road.

St John's Methodist Church

This area is known locally as Chapel Hill and is the approximate site of the old Norman Chapel that was built for Swinton. This building lasted for some 600 years and was then demolished to make way for an old Glebe house which was later converted into an infants' school in the early 19th Century. When a larger school was built the building was let as a dwelling house and was used by a family until 1911, when it was demolished. In 1913 the church hall was built at the same location.

Long since gone, but also close to this site, was once one of Swinton's oldest inns, which dated back to Medieval times.

Very little of this area has changed since 1913, which the exception of a more modern extension at the rear of the main Church, which now serves as the Church Hall.

This is the original frontage to the St. John's Wesleyan Methodist Church built close to Chapel Hill. The front section was later demolished and its present structure rebuilt, but further back off the road. Most of this church has been redeveloped, with the recent addition of a new church hall at the rear.

Very little of this area has changed (the top picture dates from 1959). The houses after the billboards have been demolished and a row of shops built. Also the old barn, on the right hidden by the trees, was once a storage building for Hurst & Sons, plumbers, but was recently demolished and several luxury flats built.

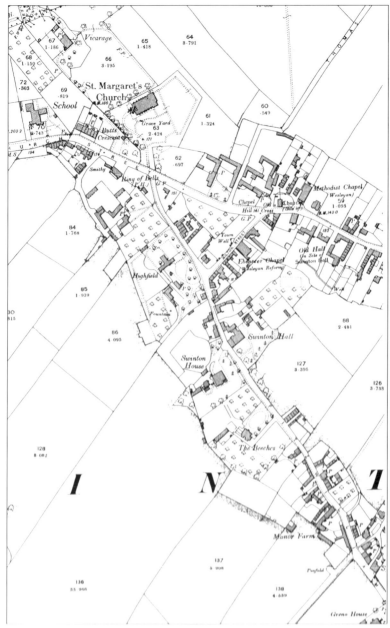

*This map shows the location of Swinton Fitzwilliam Junior and Infant
School, then takes one down Church Street towards the Ring O' Bells
public house and St. Margaret's Church and on towards Chapel Hill. To
the right you can see mention of Old Hall, where tradition states, that this
is where the favourite butler of King John (1199-1216) lived, and it is said
that the King himself slept here when on his journey from Boston to York.*

Milton Street, Fitzwilliam, Picadilly

This is opposite Chapel Hill and leads to many of the large detached and once noble houses of Fitzwilliam Street. Milton Street has changed dramatically over the years. The large house to the left of both these photographs - Milton House - has been demolished. The girl in the top picture, holding the fishes, is believed to be a servant girl from the house.

The second building is the Wesleyan Reform Chapel, and this still exists.

Left: *Milton Street today.*

This row of cottages, also on Milton Street, have also gone. Only the public house – The Travellers' Rest – still exists and that has been extensively refurbished.

The car in the picture (below) belonged to Dr. Blythman, a prominent local doctor in his day. He lived and had a surgery in a row of cottages abutting onto Milton Street, which was know locally as 'Blythman's Row'.

Fitzwilliam Street

The top part of Fitzwilliam Street, leading from Milton Street, was where the rich and affluent lived, and the large grand houses reflect this. This is the very old part of Swinton and past locals knew it as 'round the town'.

Looking in the direction of the corner of Milton Street, all the property to the right still exists. The shop at the front still remains and is one of the oldest parts of the original street. The walls to the left have gone and the area is re-developed.

An opposite view with Milton Street to the left. Most of the houses direct-ly in front have been demolished and the land is part of the Travellers' Rest gardens.

Highfield House

This large house was situated on Fitzwilliam Street and was the home of Thomas Brameld, one of the brothers who owned Rockingham Pottery. With Butler, servants and gardeners the house and adjoining gardens were kept in pris-tine fashion. When Thomas died the house was bought by Swinton Urban Council and was used by them for many decades as the Council Offices.

The gardens continued to be used by the locals. The house has been demol-ished and the gardens have sadly disap-peared with the building of Highfield Court.

Only two houses in the top photograph remain: Mirfield Cottage
to the left, believed to be the oldest cottage in Swinton, and the stone
cottage opposite with the tree outside. The remainder have all been
demolished. The row of cottages at the far end were known locally as
"Bobby's Row". It is believed this is because the first village
Policeman John Kew lived here with his family, although this is not
confirmed. These cottages have also been knocked down and Slade
Road has emerged nearby.

A later view of 'Bobby's Row' just before demolition. The road emerging from the right is Manor Road, opposite is the tree frontage of a large house known as 'The Beeches'. This house has gone and an estate has been built in its grounds still retaining its name.

The photograph above shows the affluent part of the street, looking from Milton Street. Swinton House, a large 19th Century building, is over the walled garden, to the right. This was once a club for Colliery Managers and Deputies and is now a private club. Swinton Hall is over the wall to the left. Once the home of the Brameld family, it is now converted into a series of luxury flats.

These old houses were in an area known locally as 'Monkey's Pump'. and led towards Manor Farm. They have long been demolished and a private estate built.

The Swan with Two Necks or The Gaping Goose

This three-storey building, with small cottages built to the side of it, was on Fitzwilliam Street and was once one of Swinton's oldest Coaching Inns. Both the above names are attributed to it. The cottages were once stables and coach houses before its conversion.

A well known family called Jenkinson lived here for many decades with the large house run by servants.

When the coaching inn was actually altered to a house with cottages, no one is sure. The last family to reside there was that of John Kemp - who married a Jenkinson - and the building became known, prior to its demolition, as 'Kemp's House'.

One of Swinton's oldest coaching inns The Swan with Two Necks or The Gaping Goose.

Slade Road

This is one of the many council estates that were developed in the area as the population increased. Its housing at the time was not only inadequate, but also barely habitable.

View from Fitzwilliam Street towards the town centre.

Murdered in the Execution of Duty

Prior to 1897 the area of Piccadilly was considered to be its own little hamlet and was policed from the village of Kilnhurst, however in March of that year it was able for the first time to welcome its own beat Constable, who was to work and live in the area. That Officer was PC680 John William Kew.

John originated from the Lincolnshire area and began his working life as a farm labourer. Then at the age of 21 years he sought an alternative career and joined the Lincolnshire Constabulary. Two and a half years later he applied, and was accepted by the West Riding Police. In 1896 he was transferred to Swinton Police station and six months later got his own detached beat in the mining community of Piccadilly.

Working his own area meant a 24 hour on-call commitment and the house he was given served as the Police station. He realised he could be called upon at any time to deal with any emergency and it was fully accepted that as a Policeman he should wear uniform at all times.

As with any mining community there were times when his resolve was tested, none more so than when he had to attend Middletons Villas, - the next terrace to Kew, - to deal with the Backhouse Family. Charles Benjamin Backhouse was a 23 year old miner married to Gertrude, and with a small daughter. Lodging with them was his 19 year old brother Frederick Lauder, also a miner. Domestic squabbles were regular and usually centred on allegations of Gertrude's infidelity.

In the summer of 1900 things came to a head and after one such upheaval at the Backhouse's home Frederick was reported by PC Kew, for an assault upon Gertrude, and summonsed to appear at Rotherham Magistrates Court on Monday 9th July.

Shortly after this both brothers left the house and gave up their jobs. Frederick never turned up at Court, and in his absence, was promptly found guilty, and fined.

The next day on Tuesday 10th July, Charles Backhouse went into an ironmongers on Broad Street, at Parkgate and asked the proprietor if he had any revolvers for sale. Two guns were shown to him and after selecting the largest of the two, he further purchased nine rounds of ammunition, and left.

The brothers then made their way back to Swinton, but never went home. Instead that night, just before 10 o'clock they marched into The High House pub, the only pub in the hamlet. They talked to several friends they knew, and whilst drinking Charles began showing off the gun, which was in his coat pocket. He intimated there was going to be some trouble and was heard to say 'Death or Glory' as he tapped the revolver. He was quizzed about this because the locals feared for the life of his wife but he intimated she would not be harmed and that they were not going home, but sleeping in a local field that night.

One of the neighbours became concerned about these comments and ran down Piccadilly hill and hammered on PC Kew's door. In between breaths he spilled out what he had seen and heard and suggested that it must be the Officer that Charles intended to injure, if it wasn't to be his wife, because of the summonsing of Frederick. In view of this information John Kew went looking for the Backhouse brothers.

Meanwhile after drinking up at 11 o'clock, Charles and Frederick went home with one of the friends to 74 Piccadilly. As a result of drink they ended up arguing in this house with the friend's wife, and the two brothers were ushered out of the house to calm down. As they were pushed out they were confronted by the Policeman, who appeared from round the corner. PC Kew immediately told the pair it was his intention to search them. Charles took a step backwards and to the Officer's surprise whipped out the gun. He had no time to remonstrate with Charles as a single shot blasted in Kew's direction, and he immediately doubled-up clutching at his stomach.

"What have I done to you, Charles, that you should harm me? I've never done you any harm." John moaned. Then despite his injuries he made a lunge at Charles, grabbing at his coat. At the same time Frederick grabbed for the gun, snatched it from his brothers grasp and shouted "I have one for thee you bastard." He let off another shot, which hit Kew in the leg. Frederick turned on his heels and sped from the scene, whilst Kew struggled to hold onto Charles.

Somehow the Officer managed to get his prisoner home, whilst in the meantime, news of the shooting had gone like wildfire around the hamlet. Within ten minutes a hostile crowd had surrounded the Policeman's house, baying for the Backhouse's blood.

Even though Kew was seriously injured he held onto Charles, though there was no escape for him, because of the large cordon that had formed itself around the Officer's house.

Frederick turned up to face the crowd and for reasons unknown was heard to confess 'they had both shot Kew', and even though the crowd were unsure if he was still armed or not, they detained him.

At five minutes to midnight one of the residents had made it to Swinton Police Station, about a mile away, and informed the Sergeant there, as to what had happened. Together with a number of Officers they returned to Piccadilly and secured the arrest of both Backhouse brothers. During a search of Frederick the revolver, loaded with five live rounds, was recovered from his pocket.

Doctor Fullerton, the local Practitioner, was soon at Kew's house and examined serious abdominal wounds as well as a flesh wound to the Officer's thigh. John was not despatched immediately to hospital as it would appear that previous illnesses of Kew's children had kept the family poor. This was no secret amongst the locals and they began a collection to meet the doctor's bills.

The next morning John began deteriorating slowly and Dr. Fullerton decided that the officer should go to Rotherham hospital, and he was transported by the Warren Vale Colliery ambulance. He was admitted just gone midday, but two hours later John William Kew was dead.

On Monday the 15th July the residents of Piccadilly travelled to Rotherham Court House to hear both Backhouse brothers charged with the wilful murder of PC Kew. In reply, Frederick said "Yes we did it, but we were both drunk at the time." They were consequently committed for trial and remanded to Wakefield prison.

The trial began on Friday the 27th July and many locals took the Leeds train that day. Quite a few were actually related to the Backhouse family.

All the evidence was heard in one day and by four o'clock that afternoon the jury had returned a guilty verdict of murder against Charles Backhouse and a verdict of aiding and abetting the murder against Frederick. Some of the jury requested mercy for the youngest brother.

Donning the black cap, Lord Justice Ridley, sentenced them both to death by hanging, and with stunned expressions on their faces, both condemned brothers were led away.

The jury's recommendation for mercy was duly accepted and Frederick's sentence was commuted to one of life imprisonment. However no such decision was afforded in Charles' favour and five weeks and a day after the commission of the crime the eldest brother was hanged in Armley Gaol at Leeds.

Picadilly Hill

This photograph, taken just below The High House pub, shows the view towards Kilnhurst prior to a massive building programme that began in the 1970's. The fields to the left were part of the old Roman earthwork that began at Kimberworth and worked its way through Swinton. These fields are now full of private dwellings as part of the Wentworth Parks estate.

Swinton Welfare

These photographs show the flourishing team of Bowbroom Working Men's Club, in action, on the field at Swinton Welfare. There was then a large wooden pavillion to protect one against the elements. Slightly vandalised, it lasted until the early 1960's, when it was knocked down to make way for a more modern pre-fabricated building, now used by Swinton Welfare Club.

The houses in the background are part of Park Road.

Recognise any of the local stars?

Station Street

These photographs show the view from Queen Street junction up towards Chapel Hill. Everything to the left hand side of these shots has now gone, but the buildings to the right still remain.

Above: *At the top of the street is the Glebe House (just in front of the church spire) which was built on the site of the old Norman Chapel.*
Inset: *Station Street today.*

This view, from the direction of Church Street, shows the area around Queen Street, prior to it being the centre of the town. The Barber's shop (on left) is still a Barbers today. The small street coming in from the left is hardly recognisable as Queen Street. the building beyond that was used as a very early cinema, showing lantern-type slides. It is more recognisable as the United Services Club or the 'Soldiers Club'. The smaller photograph shows the club minus triangle-shaped structure.

Queen Street

This large block of three storey houses was situated on Queen Street. The ginnel (alleyway) in the centre of these led to the workshops of the original Queen's Foundry, which was commenced in 1864 by the brothers Thomas and Charles Hattersley. In 1869 the works were moved to a larger site near to the railway on Whitelea Road. (Its current location). The foundry became very prosperous and underwent many developments, and now covers an area of 10 acres.

These houses were eventually demolished in 1936. Later the area became a car park for the new shopping precinct.

Station Street

The original Butcher's Arms (below) was at the top of the main road junction with Queen Street. It was an old low ceiling public

‌ Mexborough tramcar on Station Street. This is yet another photograph taken prior to the First ⁻ld War. This view is looking towards Queen Street and Church Street, with The United Services ‌b going out left of the picture.

house, and anyone of above average height had to bend to enter. It was demolished in the 1960's when the shopping precinct was built, and a new Butcher's Arms was constructed further back along Queen Street.

Row of shops and The Butcher's Arms just a few months before demolition.

The Picture House (above) and later the Roxy (below) was once hailed as 'the most up-to-date Picture House in the Don Valley' in 1929. When it first opened, attractions included ' The General' featuring Buster Keaton.

Sadly, dwindling numbers in the late sixties and early seventies resulted in its demise as a cinema. It lay empty for a number of years before re-opening as a centre for the craze of skate-boarding. This did not last long and quickly closed again. It was later re-opened as a squash club, and further refurbishment has now seen its development as a health gym.

The town centre photographs (above and below) were taken in 1959. In the top picture the Butcher's Arms and the shops going out towards the trees have all now been demolished for the shopping precinct and library complex.

Rock House

The main entrance to this large detached residence was from the town centre. It was originally owned and lived in by the Harrop family. In 1932 the local council purchased the house from the family, for its use as a child welfare and maternity centre. It also housed the Education Office. At the same time the Harrop's gave the gardens and grounds to be used as a haven of rest for the elderly of the area.

These grounds were always known as Harrop gardens.

In the 1960's this house and its gardens were destroyed for the rebuilding of the town centre, civic hall and library.

Station Street

The row of cottages that continued on from Harrop Gardens and down the hill. The last picture (next page) shows demolition in

progress prior to the building of the new library and gardens.

The photograph with the advertisement boards is the entrance to the private estate of Highcliffe Drive. This road used to lead to a large area of land known locally as 'the rec'.

Demolition of the row of cottages.

The photograph above shows King George V's cavalcade travelling down Swinton towards the Swinton Bridge area. It is believed their Majesty's passed through the area, having stayed with the Earl Fitzwilliam at Wentworth, and were on route to the Doncaster St. Leger race meeting.

The group of children on the embankment to the right are congregating at the location where the Swinton Victoria Club now stands.

The photograph below shows the left hand side of Station Street. The grounds of Dr. Cambells house and surgery can just be seen to the front left.

The top photograph shows the view towards the town centre, and with the exception of the tram lines, which are no longer there, very little has changed. The round edge building at the top left is the old Carnegie Library. This was erected thanks to the efforts of the Harrop family, and opened in 1906. With the opening of the new library in the shopping precinct, this has now been converted into residential flats.
Inset: Same view present-day.

This view from the railway bridge shows the junction that is now known as Lime Grove. The fencing to the left is still there, as is the 'station' public house. Wainwright's building, to the right, is now Swinton W.M.C - the 'bottom club' - as is is commonly known.

Midland Railway Station

The development of the Collieries brought the railways in abundance to the Dearne Valley, in order to move coal faster, to fuel power stations and industry, as well as homes.

The railways first came to the area as the South Yorkshire line, which ran from Barnsley to Keadby on the Trent, the station being originally what later became the Goods station. In about 1870 the Manchester, Sheffield and Lincolnshire Railway extended to Grimsby. The branch line to Sheffield was constructed, also new running sheds erected near the river. The Midland main line to London was constructed about the same period.

This photograph of engine and Midland Railway stock has been

taken looking in the general direction of Manvers Main.
The railway station was closed in the late sixties and the building is
now used by an engineering firm.
A new and more modern unmanned railway station has been built
at a location behind The Station public house.

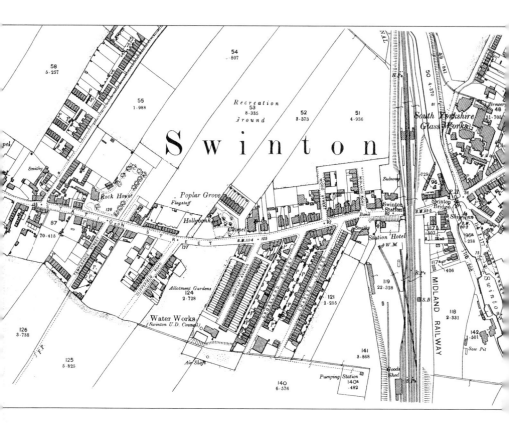

*This map shows the location of the old town centre, along Station Street,
down the hill to the Railway Station (this building is now used by a private industrial firm) and under the railway bridge into the Swinton Bridge
area, where most of the earlier 20th Century industries are situated.*

Bridge Street

The view is taken from the canal bridge looking towards the railway bridge and Station Street. It is titled 'opening of new tramways' so its date is 1907. To the right behind the horse and cart is The Canal Tavern. One can see a row of houses was attached to this public house. That row was called Canal Yard. Also in this photograph a shop canopy can be seen just before the railway bridge, to the right. There were once two shops at this location and now all that is left is a gap before the bridge. Canal Yard has also gone and is now a large car park.

The 'New Tramway Opening' is an opposite shot from the canal bridge, looking down in the general direction of Mexborough. One can see that this grand event was so important that the whole street turned out.

Since the above photograph was taken in 1959, there have been a number of changes. To the left is the entrance and sign to Dale & Brown Company. The houses with the sign no longer exist. Behind them at one time was the old slaughter house, for the three butchers on this road. They were eventually demolished for the new entrance to the bottling company. Dale & Brown sold out to United Glass in the early seventies but in 1988 the tradition of glass blowing within the town ceased as the Company closed this bottling plant. It still lies empty and derelict.

To the right, the houses, just before the Don Hotel, have also gone and a modern petrol station stands at this location.

The Red House pub, at the front, was used on a regular basis to quench the thirst of the glass blowers, across the road. It is situated on the brow of the canal bridge and across from the canal locks and because of this location it was a prop in the late 1980's for an episode of 'Last of the summer wine'. Filming caused slight chaos to the bridge area, for the best part of a week.

Swinton Bridge Street Methodist Church

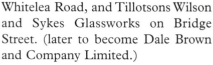

The Church first emerged in 1869 as the population increased with the development of the Collieries, Hattersley Iron Foundry on Whitelea Road, and Tillotsons Wilson and Sykes Glassworks on Bridge Street. (later to become Dale Brown and Company Limited.)

Also of note was the growing popularity of the Primitive Methodists, whose church was described as a working mans church, with influence amongst the poorer classes.

Originally the church movement held open air services in Swinton Bridge, but in 1869 a circular was sent out appealing for funds to build a new church.

Earl Fitzwilliam once again generously came to Swinton's aid and gave a plot of land to build a chapel. Its first opening ceremony took place in February 1870 and was erected next to a mineral water company, which later became Ward & Sons.

However within 20 years the services and Sunday School saw vast increases in the congregation and it was recognised greater accommodation was required. Further funds were acquired and raised and on the 14th January 1904 the new Primitive Methodist Church was built at the same location. The Church was demolished in 1969 along with many shops and houses in the Swinton Bridge location.

Pre-First World War, Bridge Street was virtually a town centre, and remained so right into the late 1950's. A lot of this area has now disappeared and on the right hand side only the Don Hotel at the far end is still standing. Right in the distance one can just see Bridge Street school.

An elderly resident who used to live in that street, can recall all the houses and businesses on the left hand side leading from Canal bridge. How many do you recall before the area was changed in the 1960's?

George Bays Tailor; Dr. Rhuarn; Jackson's fruiterers; Matthew Lowe butchers; Wardle's sweetshop; Fred Watts chemist; Carter's grocery; Drakeford bakery and Grocery; Town Row tobacconist; Primitive Methodist Chapel; Sharpley butchers; Charley Eeson barbers; Melias grocers; Dorothia Allen (house); Heeley cobbler; Fieldhouse butchers; Dorothia Alien's sweetshop; Swindler's electrical shop; Barton's fish shop; Hanson's butchers; Helliwell's fruit and fish; White's newsagents; Harrison's grocers; Fisher's Ladies outfitters; Sherwood's cobblers; Nettleton's off-licence; Carr's butchers.

Bridge Street, facing in the direction of Mexborough. The Don Hotel, although now refurbished, still exisits, as do the row of terraced homes

Bridge Street school, constructed to accommodate the workers children that flooded into the area at the turn of the century as the Collieries and other industries developed.. This is where local celebrity Tony Capstick played his first pranks.

The Swinton end of Whitelea Road's housing stock finally disappeared in the 1970's and this area now carries a lot of small industrial units. At one time the road had several streets, St.Michael's Church and Zion chapel, and the local school children were taught at Bridge Street School.

The photograph below shows a row of terraces which led on from Queen's foundry.

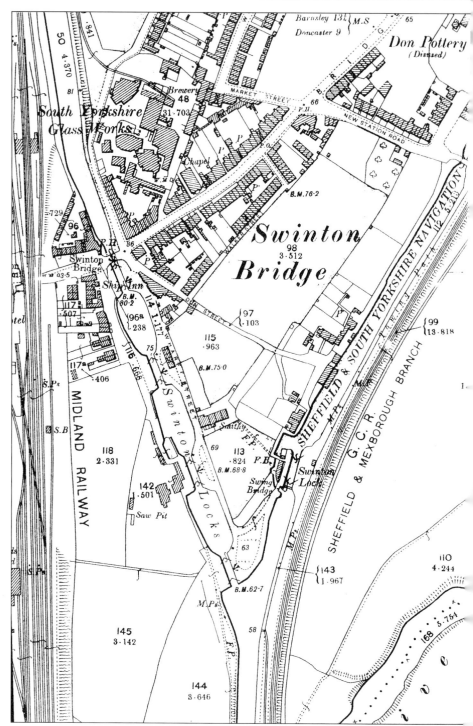

This map shows the industrial section of Swinton fromcanal bridge and down towards the Don pottery, which leads into Mexborough.

The Mexborough and Swinton Traction Company

An electricity supply came to Swinton in 1898 and three years later. The Mexborough and Swinton Traction Company agreed to pay the District Council for the transfer of the Electric Lighting Order, in order that they could run their newly acquired tram buses to Swinton.

The supply for these new trams was by direct current, which came from the Tramways own Power Station, housed in what is now the workshops for bus overhauling, at Dale Road, Rawmarsh.

There was just one underground cable on a main route from Rawmarsh, along Warren Vale, to Swinton, and the original stud-contact system actually resulted in animals being electrocuted.

The first line opened on the 1st February 1907, with a service of open top double deck tramcars. That same year, on the 3rd August, the line was extended through Swinton, to the old toll bar at Mexborough.

The electric trolley bus system, quickly developed over the next few years and became much extended, also updating it with an overhead lines network.

However in 1954, because of ever increasing costs, a decision was taken to cease any further development of this system, in favour of

Station Street, Swinton.

newly tested and purchased diesel motor buses.

A higher capacity single deck bus was successfully introduced and found favour with both passengers and staff, and subsequently, the last public service of trolley buses was operated on March 26th 1961.

The following set of photographs show trams and trolley buses at several locations throughout Swinton during various stages of the operations of Mexborough and Swinton Traction Company.

Not everything was smooth running for the company in the early days. In July 1908 the photograph (left) was taken when a tram slid off the rails and crashed down the embankment on Warren Vale Road. Although there were injuries, fortunately none were fatal.

The photograph (below), also taken in the early days of the company, shows employees in exceptionally fine uniforms posing for the camera. This was taken at the depot at Rawmarsh, which is still in use as a bus depot.

Warren Vale (view from Rawmarsh looking towards Swinton) Station Street .

Woodman roundabout

Station Street. The road to the left leads to Swinton Railway Station. the Station building is now a private engineering firm.

Bridge Street. The Canal Tavern House stands to the left.

The bridge spans over the canal at Swinton locks, where Waddingtons boat-yard is situated.

There are three public houses in the area of the bridge. To the left is the Canal Tavern, the one over the bridge in the photographs opposite is the Red House and the large building to the right (bottom photo) is the Ship Inn on Wharf Lane. All these pubs were used regularly at one time to quench the thirst of many boatmen who operated on this stretch of the canal (which has now dried up) as well as the Glass blowers from Dale & Browns bottling Company.

The ghost of a former landlord who died in the Ship Inn is said to haunt the premises. A previous tenant fled from the premises and called in the clergy to exorcise the apparition, after toilets mysteriously flushed and doors closed fast.

Street, Swinton.

A lot of the area has changed, almost the entire left-hand side has now been demolished and a modern petrol station has been built. Many of the shops to the right, however, still exist.

Below a photograph of Rowms Lane.

Canal at Bowbroom

This photograph is taken overlooking Bowbroom bridge. The canal ran from Wath through Manvers Main Colliery complex and linked up at Waddington Lock and boatyard with the Don navigation. It was used in the main to transport coal from the pit to industry at Rotherham and Sheffield.

In the summer, local youths from the area used this canal frequently to swim and bathe.

The photograph was taken in 1953. Today only the railway line is in existence.

Manvers Coking Plant

It seemed at one time that because all heavy industry used coal, that there was always going to be 'the pits'. Moreover we all had coal fires in our homes, which was used for cooking as well as heating.

Swinton and the local towns grew with the advent of the Collieries, as more and more flooded into the area for work in the mines.

The work was physically demanding in grimy conditions, and dangerous and it bred a unique breed of men.

The Coking Plant was part of the Manvers Main Colliery and provided hundreds of jobs locally. However the late 1980's were a disaster for the area as it saw the massacre, not only of the'pits', but of jobs, and a way of life.

The Coking Plant was part of that demise, and in a relatively short period of time of it being vacated, it was demolished.

Now this area is being regenerated by the Dearne Valley partnership. European funding has developed smaller and newer industries, and a road system has been carved through, what was once, the Manvers Main complex.

Manvers Main Rail Disaster

Local witnesses watched in horror as the London – Bradford express, plunged down an embankment, near to Manvers Main Colliery, killing many on board. The majority of passengers were returning from their Whitsuntide holiday break.

The two-engined train had travelled from St.Pancras station when it hit distorted rails, caused by the heat of the sun at the top of the thirty foot incline. The engines rocked and buckled, before carriage

upon carriage smashed into one another. As it ground to a halt eight people were dead and 55 were injured, many seriously.

At the subsequent inquest, tribute was paid to the men of Manvers Main Colliery and local doctors and residents, who crawled amongst the wreckage to rescue passengers. The Colliery ambulance room was used as an emergency clearing station, prior to transporting them to Mexborough Montagu hospital.

Rescue work carried on all through the night and the only visible lighting was from the glare of the giant bleeder flame from the colliery yard.

SHEETS
HEAVY TWILLED SHEETS
Unbleached, 80 x 100.
6 coupons. Each   14/6
WHITE COTTON SHEETS
80 x 100.
6 coupons. Each   14/6
WHITE COTTON SHEETS
80 x 100.
6 coupons. Each   13/7
Butterfields
OF BARNSLEY

HEAD
SQUARE
HAND PAINTED SQUARES
in pretty pastel shades, for holiday wear.
2 coupons   37/-
JACQMAR SQUARES in the newest designs and colourings. Now displayed on ground floor.
Butterfields
OF BARNSLEY

South Yorkshire Times
and
Mexborough & Swinton Times.
Established 1877.   SATURDAY, MAY 22, 1948.   PRICE THREEPENCE

Heavy Casualties in Rail Crash

HAVOC FOLLOWS WATH DERAILMENT

Coaches Plunge Into Pit Yard

LONDON—BRADFORD EXPRESS MEETS WITH CATASTROPHE

[BY OUR OWN REPORTER]

A WATH MAN, MR. BEN WILLIAMSON, OF 27, ASH ROAD, WHO SAW TUESDAY'S LONDON-BRADFORD EXPRESS DISASTER, RUSHED ACROSS THE MANVERS MAIN COLLIERY BY-PRODUCT PLANT YARD,

The Earl Fitzwilliam

Since the middle of the 19th century the Fitzwilliam family have been involved in funding the many developments of Swinton, and though there will be no more Earls to continue the family name, their legacy will always remain with the street and school name.

In this photograph the main Earl benefactor of the area is seen with the Bishop of Sheffield consecrating the earth within the grounds of St. Margaret's Church, for the stone laying of Swinton's Memorial Cross in remembrance of its losses during the First World War.

The Eighth Earl of Fitzwilliam

The double tragedy struck the area over the Whitsuntide break of 1948, with the untimely death of Peter, Lord Fitzwilliam. He was killed when his light aeroplane went out of control and crashed over France. At the time he was with his girlfriend, Lady Hartington, who was the daughter of Joseph Kennedy, the U.S Ambassador to this country. Two other occupants in the plane also lost their lives.

He was the last son in direct line to the Fitzwilliam estate and in a farewell tribute, thousands lined Wentworth in mourning, as he was laid to rest in the shadow of the Parish Church.

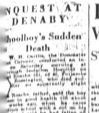

NQUEST AT
DENABY
hoolboy's Sudden
Death

EARL'S VILLAGE - FUNERAL
Vast Concourse of Mourners
STRIKING MANIFESTATION OF
DISTRICT'S REGARD

SOUTH YORKSHI

National Federa
Decorator

IMPORTANT N

Whitsuntide Walks

"Does tha like me new clothes for Whit Missus?" This was the familiar cry of children country-wide as they and their parents formed part of the community and Church groups, as they congregated together for the annual walks around their respective towns.

Swinton was no exception as the local townsfolk gathered in their Whitsuntide best attire to walk through the town. The walk would begin in the Swinton Bridge area and grow as it made its way through the main town, finally finishing on the large fields of the old rectory, at the rear of St. Margaret's Church. There, after a short ceremony, the throng engaged in sporting and fun events in a gala like atmosphere, until early evening.

These two photographs, taken in 1937 sh The Swinton Primitive Methodist Sunda School group (left) prior to the commencement of the Whit Walk and belo the group at its final stage near the rector fields.

43

Robert Fowler

Engineer and Surveyor to Swinton Urban District Council

It feels only right that I should mention Mr. Robert Fowler, not just because he was my great-grandfather, but also as a testimony to some of the work he involved himself in to develop Swinton during the Victorian era.

He was born, the son of a farmer and originated from Gravely in Cambridgeshire. However he never followed the farming path as expected, for his heart and mind were filled with wider visions. A quick and eager learner, he trained as a Surveyor and Engineer, and his first association with Yorkshire was in 1883 at the age of 23 years.

In that year he took up post as assistant engineer in the town of Hull and developed his skills on the construction of the Alexandra dock.He later went on to involve himself in the building and construction of the Thornton and Keighley railway at Bradford.

That work took up ten years and as an experienced 33 year old, he secured post as the Engineer and Surveyor for Swinton Urban Council.

Until the latter part of the nineteenth century, Swinton had no mains water supply, the population having to rely on springs, wells and streams.Then in 1878 a scheme was introduced for supplying the area with piped water.

Robert became the district Surveyor in 1893 and was involved in developing the last part of the scheme, linking up water and drainage pipes to supply property around the Woodman, Rockingham Road and Swinton Common. He served Swinton for sixteen years before retiring from public service to practise in his own Engineering and Surveying business, within the Rycroft area of Rawmarsh.

The small fortune he generated allowed him to retire at the age of 58 to live on his own property at Dolcliffe Vale, Mexborough, where he also owned the roller skating rink. He also owned terraced housing on Rowms Lane and Talbot Road, which he rented to local families.

Locally he was looked upon as a man of wide experience and good business judgement and his love of horticulture became much in evidence through his surveying work. He developed the initiative of planting trees throughout the district to beautify the town. He was also a strong supporter of open spaces for all and used his status within the community to encourage the building of parks and playgrounds.

He never actually retired as such from public life as he offered himself as a candidate for Mexborough Council, and was successful first time. He later went on to Chair the District Council.

At the age of 79 yrs he died and was buried in a family grave at St. Margaret's Church.

The Don Pottery

The Don Pottery was founded shortly before 1800, and was close-ly situated adjoining the wharf, at the bottom of Swinton near Mexborough. Although lesser known, it has been described 'as probably one of the most interesting in Yorkshire.'

Once again it was the Green family from Leeds, who then had links with the Swinton Pottery,who initially funded this Pottery. They purchased large amounts of waste land and with the aid of partners set about erecting a new Pottery.

The products they made and sold were very similar to pottery ware they were already making at the other businesses they owned, and at its height it was employing some 300 local people. But the family suffered substantial losses during the break out of the French war, and they were forced to sell this Pottery as well as the others they owned.

So in 1834 Mr Samuel Barker, a local businessman of the nearby Mexborough old Pottery, bought it and continued to produce

The dilapidated buildings left behind from the Don Pottery. They have now been demolished, the last occupant of the area was a scrap dealer. The photograph to the left shows a fine example of one of the potteries many wares.

Pottery, adding new designs and products. His old Pottery closed in 1844, but he continued his operations at The Don Pottery.

Production continued at these works until 1893, but as at so many potteries, the standard of workmanship and design declined. At one stage they were trading with Russia and the Americas but unfortunately those markets dried up and seven years before the dawn of the 20th Century the works closed.

Memoirs of a Swinton elder

As a final post-script to this book I would like to reproduce text from the memoirs of a Swinton resident who never officially had her work published. Miss Vickers was a long-time teacher at the original Fitzwilliam School and has only recently died. I have already used her childhood memories of the great fire at St. Margaret's Church and after reading her early recollections, I thought it apt to conclude with her infant vision of Swinton:

"There was always a large rookery, much larger than at present, on the south side of the Church, hence the name Rookery Road. At the corner, which is now a garden, was a huddle of about 12 to 15 small cottages always called "The Rookery", three of them facing the street, well below street level. The road leading to Central Avenue and Park Road was the cart track to Highfield Farm. The smithy was next door to the Ring-O-Bells and together with the yard in front of it occupied the space in front of the shop. On warm summer days we sat in school at our lessons and all the doors and windows were open so we often heard the clip clop of horses' hooves and the ring of the anvil.

Between the Church and the Gate Inn were about 20 cottages including the little old Toll Bar House, now pulled down, and one man whom I knew very well and who was for many years a sidesman at Church remembered the Toll Gates being there but not in use.

After the Gate Inn the road to Wath was a lovely country lane, with a long row of beautiful beech trees along the right-hand side and also many other trees - elm, oak, sycamore and I remember just one Spanish chest-

nut. On the other side was one cottage, now occupied by
Mr. Lockyer and his family, but it stood in the middle of
a field, and right at the top of the road was nothing but
fields, both arable and pasture. About half way up on
that side was 'Jimmy's Lane' leading to the farm and
out into Warren Vale Road, which was just a country
lane from Woodman Corner, right down into Wath village. Darwyn Avenue and also part of Romwood were
once a lovely wood which in the Spring was just a beautiful carpet of bluebells.

Rockingham Road was another country lane with a
few stone-built cottages in it. Where the large roundabout is now there were two narrow lanes cutting each
other at right angles.

The pottery field was a wonderful playground for
children. There were two ponds where we could gather
frogspawn or a bit later tadpoles, tiddlers and stickle-
backs. The large round pond in the middle was the
favourite. We rarely went near the smaller one a bit
higher up on the right and the one we always called the
' hot water pond'.

I've been told that both ponds were made for use by
the Rockingham Pottery when it was working. The
smaller one had a steam pipe going into it and the
water was a degree or so warmer than the other, hence
the name 'hot water pond'.

When we wanted to pick flowers we had a large and
varied choice. I remember an old kiln and chimney
standing, the remains of an old pottery. They were in a
very dilapidated state and were taken down some years
ago for safety reasons. There were also three old cottages in the field and one in Pancheon Field next to the
pottery.

This is practically all there was of Swinton, above
Saint Maraget's Church when I was a child. We've stood
in the schoolyard and seen hounds in full cry. We've also
watched sparrow hawks hovering and swoop down on
their prey below, and in Summer time several skylarks
were often singing and soaring into the blue".

Do you remember any of these local adverts?